Sweet Sounds of Life

Sweet Sounds
of Life

Poems by
Janelle Carman Lapaglia

Exposition Press   Hicksville, New York

To my mother, Arbra Carman, who has been my inspiration over the years, and to my husband, Louis, and our children, who encouraged me to publish my poems

First Edition

© 1979 by Janelle Carman Lapaglia

ISBN 0-682-49332-5

Printed in the United States of America

Contents

For a Child Gone

I wondered, as I gazed upon the coffin
Where the small child lay,
This God of love, this God of mercy,
What would he say?
Pain ripping through my body,
My heart filled with agony,
God, where are you? I say—where is
Peace, love, and harmony?
Yesterday, yes, bring it back,
Please, just once again.
I want to hear the laughter,
See the special way he grins,
To feel the warmth of his tiny fingers
As he takes me by the hand.
So many things I long for, Lord,
To see him as a man.
I know he is in your keeping now, and
You will take away my fears.
The memories of a precious angel I'll
Have throughout my years.
And after the hurt and pain are gone I know I'll
Thank you so
For lending him to us for a while,
Letting us see him grow.

September

I watched the morning dawning on that
September day,
Thinking on the beauty God gives in
So many ways.
Soon the trees would change their
Color;
The breeze would suddenly be much cooler.

The beauty of the season, not changed by any
Man:
Spring with its blossoming beauty throughout
The land;
Summer filled with laughter as the
World enjoys the sun;
Fall comes and brings us rest from
All the summer fun.
So much beauty God brings in each
Season—
Each has a purpose; each change is for
A reason.

Land of Beautiful People

In a dream I saw a field of beautiful flowers
All in bloom;
I looked as far as I could see, all so bright
With no gloom,
As if the whole world were covered with all the
Flowers that grew.
Each color seemed to complement the other as
I gazed upon the view.
Some were tall and straight, while others
Were somewhat small and round—
So many different flowers, yet all were
Growing from the ground.
I could not choose which were the most lovely
That day,
For all were beautiful and special in their own
Kind of way.
I wanted to go out into the field and walk,
To touch each plant,
But the distance was so great, I could only
Touch a few, then just glance.
When I awoke I could plainly see my view
Was really a world full of people I wish I knew.
Each color was so perfect as it shone in the field;
None was any prettier than the other—each was
    God's will.
Each color, stature, and form was complementary to
The other.
What a beautiful sight to see each one
As our brother!
To know that none was created to be
Superior, that some may boast,
But we are all a beautiful garden of
Flowers at the most.

11

Struggling One

Oftentimes the fight is not really with
Anyone,
Just some growing pains within, a battle
To be won.
A challenge comes as life in its reality must
Be faced,
Not simple by any means, but off we go
In haste—
Out to make our mark in society, to
Change the world, it seems,
Only to find this impossible; it was all
Just a dream.
So the struggle lingers but eases as we
Understand:
Time and wisdom work their course
And make for a better man.

Our Son

I watched with sad but grateful heart as
He walked beside the girl,
Knowing his life was changing—he was entering
Another world,
Leaving behind him mom and dad and
Things that once meant all,
Embarking upon life in full force, for he
Had heard the call.
How can I tell him of all the joys life
Can bring
Without telling of all the wicked worldly
Schemes?
He alone must tread the road of life with
All the good and bad,
Eliminating failures, originating success,
Clinging to hope as he's led.

A Growing

The child was desperately trying to hold
His own,
Enjoying the privilege of family and home.
Even without knowing his world was
Expanding,
Growing mentally and physically as his
Body demanded,
Restless he became trying to shake
Away the binds.
Unaware of what was happening, this
Would take more time,
Along with love, anguish, this unexplainable
Force,
For nurturing within, an individual was
Emerging forth,
Breaking loose from the imitation of
Mom and dad and those close by,
To be a combination of environment
And that unique something inside.

Only Yesterday

I saw her eyes swollen with tears
Beckoning,
Trying hard to face one more day as
Dawn was breaking,
Wandering aimlessly from one problem
To face another—
Would this day somehow be different
From the others?
I searched for words of comfort to pass
On to her,
Hoping to help in some way to show
Her how much I cared.
Memories, oh, the memories were so much
The same:
The past I'd lived, so much wrong, so much
Pain;
The burning tears my heart began to
Sink.
Only yesterday, only yesterday—I have
Only God to thank.

God Paints a Rainbow

When the rain stopped falling,
I could see up in the heavens
God painting a rainbow—a promise he had given.
The same is true with life—the rain won't stay for
long,
For God will paint a rainbow; he'll send a brand-new
song.
God never leaves or forsakes us once we let him in,
Though our days are often cloudy and the rain he
sometimes sends.
He is always beside us, watching, ready to lend a
hand,
Ready to paint a rainbow, as only God can.

In God's Care

The rain stopped and I walked outside
To see God's creation so much alive.
I wanted to run out and touch each thing,
To soak up the beauty brought out by the rain,
To see, to feel, as if by this I could capture
The worth
Of just one small beauty on this great earth.
The rain washed the plants so gracefully;
The breeze dried them most gently.
I looked, I touched, I smelled, and with all
My might,
I tried to capture for a moment the beauty
Of this precious sight,
For God was taking care of all his creation,
Not just for you and me, but for all the
Nations.

16

The Tree with Outstretched Arms

The tree seemed to spread its beautiful
Arms around the house,
As though to shelter us and keep all
Harm out.
The leaves, as they began to sprout
So tiny and green,
Gave the house a warm, beautiful, protective
Scene.
As the color changed and the leaves began
To fall,
With the pitter-patter of tender love the tree
Would call.
The leaves now on our roof and beneath
Our feet,
The tree's still tall with outstretched arms
Never answering to defeat,
Here to care and watch over our home
Forever.
The tree with outstretched arms seems
To hold our home together.

My Search Ended

I searched for honesty, oh, to find someone
Sincere,
Someone who by nature was honest, kind,
And dear,
Someone with heartfelt emotions, not
From the shoulder pretense
That soon would fade as the sunset to
Dark intense.
I needed security of a man that knew his
Will and mind,
Someone not easily conquered by the
Crafty, worldly kind,
A man who stood on his honor and strived
For all life could give,
Watching out for his fellowman, never
Boasting of the righteous way he lived.
The day came—God had heard my
Constant plea.
My search ended, for God sent you to me—
More than in my limited thoughts that I did ask,
For I never dreamed anyone could beat the task,
Honest, kind, and true, someone on whom to
Rely,
Yet strong as the mountains against yonder
Sky.

Two Worlds

I watched you as for work you dressed.
I was envious, I'm sorry to confess.
You walked with ease and assurance,
Knowing your capabilities—your endurance,
Ready to meet the world with its demands.
I was left home with the children to command.

Together

The unheard words, the unseen gestures,
The many things you do,
The love you give, withholding nothing,
Just being you,
Love growing as our minds and hearts,
Feeling not as two but one,
Needing only each other, content when
Day is done,
No more searching, no empty rooms,
No lonely wasted days—
You and I against the world,
Together, now and always.

On Loving

I saw your eyes and I knew kindness.
I touched your hand and grasped assurance.
I felt your lips and tasted love.
You spoke and I became real.

Sixteen

Today you're sixteen; the long-awaited day has
Finally arrived.
You feel grown-up, your spirit free—you're so
Much alive.
Your thinking is changing, as you're forced to
Mature.
Decisions, pressures seem too much to endure.
But as the problems come and each is solved,
A new door is opened, your life more involved,
For each problem has an answer, as you knew it
   would—
Each problem veils some hidden truth that must
   eventually
Be understood;
So search in your years of youth for wisdom
And understanding.
Depend on your creator for guidance, for he is love
And never demanding.
When all of life seems to tumble in upon you,
Only God will provide you strength to see you
   through.
So while you're young and before many mistakes are
   made,
Put God in command, so you need not be afraid.
The earth is the Lord's and the fullness thereof;
He with infinite understanding guides us by his love.

A Mother's Prayer

The children are playing outside my door,
Joys of laughter I just adore.
O Lord, let this day be a memory for me.
Soon they will grow up, no more on my knee.
Help me to prepare them for the future so bleak,
To turn them over to you to guide and keep.
I'm selfish to want them always with me.
Your plans are perfect; I must obey thee,
Give you the children to work out your plan—
I pray for wisdom so I may understand.

A Mother's Cry

I heard a cry from a mother who was
Filled with hurt.
The children she had tenderly caressed and
Loved from the first
Were now rebelling, cursing their heritage,
Denying their God!
The memories of a mother's kiss on a tear-filled
Face forgot,
No thoughts toward the future, no thoughts
Of the past,
Just searching a thrill for the moment,
Nothing that would last.
Oh, mother, where will they go from here?
Must you always live with this terrible fear?
What happened to this child as he grew
Independent?
Was it destined by his generation; were
We too lenient?

21

God's Gifts

God gave me a family so beautiful and
Sweet.
I thank him each day for a life so
Complete.
Tho oftentimes I wonder why he blessed me so,
I accept with grace these blessings bestowed.

In Your Stead

I prayed in your stead this morning;
I knew you were rushed for time.
Maybe the Lord would understand and accept my
    prayer,
For I am thine.
I praised him first for you and your
Wondrous ways to me.
In humble adoration I praised both him and thee.
After my prayer was ended I knew he answered
Right then,
For he realized I loved you only less than him.

Black Is Beautiful

Have you ever seen anything more beautiful
Than a scene outlined in black?
Or a beautiful black raven full speed in flight?
A black night filled with a thousand stars
And the moon?
If you've never thought of black as beautiful,
Look at a black child soon.

Without a Doubt

If you were to ask me why my God allows the hurt
   and pain,
Why in times of sorrow we can't see the sunshine,
Only the rain,
I would not know the answers and yet I know
Without a doubt,
My Savior loves me and that's what
Makes me shout.
Standing near a mother, as they lay her son to rest,
Or trying to comfort the father as against God he
   protests,
Watching as they pull bodies from the wreckage of
A storm,
Feeling for the survivors as they hang their heads
   and mourn,
Yet God in all his love and mercy sent us
His saving grace,
Sent his only son, so he might take our place;
So when I see the hurt, the awful sin of pain,
I cling more closely to the Savior and true to
Him remain.
Although I don't know the answers, I know
   Without a doubt,
Someday I'll reign with him in glory and that's
Why I shout.
Relying on his promise, I wait for him each day,
Just waiting for the promise to take me home to stay.

God's Love

The sun shining bright, illuminating all God's
  creations,
Shining down into the darkest sea and deep into
  vegetation,
Reflecting God's created beauty, nowhere it cannot
  go,
Bringing out the glorious beauty, giving earth its
  glow . . .
The love of God reflects our life with the same
  illuminating force.
No limits or restrictions, it pours from an unlimited
  source.

The Most Beautiful People

The most beautiful people
That walk upon this earth
Are those that have settled for
Nothing less than second birth,
The ones who have the wisdom
To accept with simple faith
That God, their creator,
With love has provided grace.

A God So Great

I have knelt before God at the throne of grace,
Wept in his presence as I visioned his face,
Marveled at the concern he would have for me,
A God so great he made the earth and sea,
Trembled as his spirit filled my soul with assurance,
His love to lead and guide through each endurance.

God Is Not Apart

God is not apart, somewhere we must search.
Instead he's in our hearts, where emotions are
  kindled first.
He is not somewhere in the distant skies,
Where we must wonder if he hears our cries,
Not by distance that we can measure,
Yet in our hearts that we may treasure
The very being of Christ so easy to reach,
As the wind blows at will the spirit repeats.
God is so near yet we treat him apart,
Forgetting his spirit is present in our hearts.

Another Day

He went to work this morning
Much against my will.
I thought I'd try to convince him
At home he was needed still.
But as I was about to make my plea,
On the desk stacked neatly I saw
The reason he must flee.

Brave New World

The cruelty of the world sometimes hangs
Over us on every hand.
Confusion often covers our compassion,
And fear is in command.
Our attitudes change; our minds are no
Longer open, but biased.
Hearts are sad, merriment long forgotten,
Principles are unadvised.
Bitterness surges forth, morals altered at
Our leisure,
Principles tossed aside for gain, morals
Dropped for pleasure.

On Stage

We each are born for a reason, a purpose for our
Existence.
Each has his role to play, as soon as birth
Makes its entrance.
The stage is set; the act begins, sometimes winners,
Sometimes losers.
As life begins to unfold and the plot is exposed,
We realize we are the choosers.

Don't Worry

Don't worry about tomorrow, I hear
People say.
I'll try not to, but, gee—look at me
Today.
Yesterday I sat, had tea, and moped
About;
Today I wish I'd worried just enough
To clean the house.

Dilemma

As lonely as the sunset as it beckons
Its last call,
The dilemma of the young girl arising
From the fall,
As the sun again will rise and touch
The height above,
The tender heart must rise, summoned
By her love.
Plagued by the haunting memories,
She rises as before
To reach a new plateau as she enters
Another door.
And so life goes, repeating as through its
Nature's courses
The flow of life continues, guided by surrounding
Forces.

Life Goes By So Fast

Life goes by so fast, it seems,
We hardly have time to wish or dream.
Just rush from morning till night is coming,
Then hurry to sleep to rest for the morning,
To start all over again with haste:
Not stopping to think of the waste.
Think of the pleasure of a walk along the beach,
Or picnicking on a cool, winding creek,
Driving carefree on the country roadside,
Watching the squirrels scamper off to hide,
Enjoying life God planned so great;
Let's slow down and live before it's too late!

Talks

I strolled down the path today,
Near the old house not far away.
The cold wind was blowing on my back.
I kicked the ice and watched it crack.
Memories came back as I walked,
Remembering you, the times we talked,
Dreams we had as we lived here.
Life was simple, without care.
Now I watch the ice crack beneath my feet,
See my life, as in a mirror, it repeats,
The many pieces scattered here and there,
Gathering my life as the pieces to repair.

Express One's Self

Sometimes to express yourself is so
Revealing,
But how wonderful to tell others of your
Feelings,
To open your heart and your mind,
To share with others the joys you find!
Thought and feeling seem to come alive,
As they are brought from the heart into sight.

Another Time

The house looked so deserted as I
Passed by it today.
The laughter was gone, no children out
To play.
The little bush beside the steps was
All but buried,
Seems like such a short time ago
When near it we would tarry . . .
So sad to see how time has changed
Things so,
As different people we become,
As different places we go.

Time with God

Quietness amid the noisy day,
The times I pause quietly to pray,
The noise heavy on every hand,
The world making its demands,
In the midst of it all,
Moments with God I lovingly recall.

Emotions

Life is full of deep emotions,
Some so tender, others commotion.
Our minds wondering wildly,
As the heart obeys its call.
A human so complex, a being
Wandering—somehow not seeing—
Needing, wanting, hoping still
His life with love be filled.

Questions

I've searched for answers to questions
Of life that arise,
Dig deep in my mind and on my heart
Sometimes rely.
Emotions are kindled as I constantly look
For answers to questions I can't find in books.

Christmas Joy

Christmas is a time of celebration,
A time of truth and dedication,
A time for snow and lighted trees,
Excited children filled with glee,
Bells chiming, choirs singing,
Busy streets, windows gleaming.
Santa's coming; stockings are hanging.
Christmas is a time for celebrating.

Sweet Sounds of Life

It was quiet in the house today.
I opened wide the curtains and the window partway.
All around me were soundless objects, no movement.
The children in school, I miss the sound of enjoyment.
The birds were lined on the wire across the way.
The dog lay against the gate waiting to play.
Soon the children will return and noise will
Fill the room.
The birds will again sing, the day lose
Its gloom.

Missing You

I woke up this morning
Thinking of you,
Wishing somehow to see you,
Feeling that you were blue.
I fixed breakfast wondering
If you had eaten,
Got dressed,
Picking something I thought you'd like,
Opened the door
And listened to the birds sing,
Hoping you were looking out
And enjoying this beautiful spring.
I walked outside,
Picked a rose, and as I held it near,
I wondered if you really knew
How much I care.
I wanted to bring it to you
For you to see and touch,
A tender rose, a warm day,
And missing you so much.

Just Clay

Life is lived in complex dramas,
Acted out as best we can.
New scenes bring forth new actors,
New scenery as our life demands.
Always in our dramas
We play the leading role,
Our emotions being put in full demand,
Often beyond control,
Hardly time to know what to
Say or do.
Some acts we plan, but so many
We fall into,
No time to prepare—just live as they occur,
Not knowing how our peers
Or the critics will concur,
Trusting not ourselves nor any man to arrange
Our play,
Remembering that God is the potter
We the clay.

Help Me, Lord

My life is but a memory to those I've known,
The way I've lived, the seeds I've sown.
Help me, Lord, your life to share with those I know,
To sow seeds that will help them grow.
Help me hold my light high, that others may see
The joy of love that comes through serving thee.
Help me not to lose control, to say a word
In haste,
That my life to others won't be a waste.

The Water

The water splashed with great force
Against the rocky shore.
As my mind churned and turned,
Reality seemed no more.
As the water drifted back
Out into the troubled sea,
My soul I began to search,
So I might find the me
That once was bright and happy
With such a desire to live.
Somewhere once I knew myself
And had so much to give.
As the water finds its way
From between the rocks and sand,
My mind must also find its way
Back to higher lands.

Spring Long Gone

A robin came by to visit, to tell me spring was
    coming.
I noticed a flower—over it a bird was humming.
The beauty of spring before my eyes flashed.
As a picture of newness, freshness, I wish spring
    would last.
Summer came, which was only spring more mature,
To give us strength, for fall we knew was near.
Then winter came, the days so cold and long,
But beauty filled our hearts, remembering the spring
    long gone.

Spring

Spring is coming; I feel it in the air.
The anticipation of the moment is everywhere.
The gloominess of the winter is giving way.
Spirits are lifted as they welcome the day.
Nature cries out, grieving no more.
Farewell to winter—spring I adore!

Drought

The land is barren,
Not a tree to be seen,
The blazing, blistering heat,
The land so lean,
Aching for the rain, to be blessed
With a stream,
Crying for a little life,
So beauty might be seen.

I Love You

I see you in everything, my love,
The sun, the rain, the sky above,
A flower's blossom in the spring,
A crowded beach that summer brings,
The chilling breeze brought in by fall,
Logs on the fire as winter calls.
I see you in good times, in bad times too.
I see you in everything—'cause I love you.

Friend

This morning a friend came by for tea,
A lovely morning filled with noises
From the sea.
We sat and talked of everything from A to Z.
How sad life would be without a friend
And a cup of tea.

So Little Time

So little time we give to those
Who really need a word or so.
We rush to make ourselves look great,
But overlook and not an effort make
To help a friend who needs a smile.
We neglect the things that are so worthwhile.

Ravaged

Huge mountains of aged rocks lay outstretched
On either hand,
Barren as the desert, except for a few trees
Sprinkled on the land.
Reaching high were rocks that were twisted
And tangled.
Nature with its constant forces has left it
Old and mangled.

Nature's Beauty

The snow rippled from the high mountain
Peak,
Forming the streams that sparkle beneath
My feet,
Nature in its beauty unfolding with
Never-ending forces,
Boasting, as it changes, of its unlimited
Sources.

The Spirit of Joseph

Lord, give me the spirit of Joseph of old,
Who loved you, Lord, even when he was sold.
How in prison he walked and talked with you,
Although he was there for something he didn't do.
He could have been bitter with such a load,
But he took it all to you; Joseph was bold.
Lord, give me the spirit of Abraham who
Was faithful in all things.
When told his son would be his sacrifice
To bring,
He trusted and did as you told him he
Should.
He didn't ask why, or maybe he would.
He followed your will all the way through.
Give me this spirit, so to you I can be true.
Give me the spirit of Job who had patience
To see things through,
Never gave up, although this seemed the thing
To do,
But waited and prayed when friends couldn't
Be found.
He didn't give up, lying sick on the ground.
Give me this spirit, Lord, that I may see
The joy, peace, and love that comes
Through serving thee.

Time

"Time waits for no man"
Has often been repeated.
It's true that man must
Conquer time as needed.
The moments tick away,
Regardless, never changing.
Time is given
For our maintaining.
Seconds sometimes can
Change the tide.
We may be foolish,
But time can't be denied.
Wasted moments can't be restored,
Neither sooner or later,
Without neglecting something else,
Which might be greater.

Desert Drive

We drove across the desert of barren
Waste and sand,
Hoping soon to leave it and find a
Better land.
Nothing could grow;
No life could there be.
I studied the distance as far as
I could see.
This—I thought, is the way our lives
Could turn,
If we were not loved nor gave love in
Return.
As the drifting sands, our lives would
Drift about,
Searching for the love that man can't
Live without.

Linger, Thanksgiving Day

The house is warm, not from the logs
Heaped upon the flame,
Nor from the sun flickering through the
Narrow windowpane,
But from the hearts of those dear,
Who have laughed and loved and lived,
Who've shared throughout the years,
Their hopes, their joys—love they give.
So I pray—Oh, linger, spirit of Thanksgiving Day.
Bring us this warmth, the love, that it may stay.
Linger on when the way is rough and times so
Bleak,
Thanksgiving ever in our hearts to share
And keep.

Mother's Song

The mountains stood hard and cold,
Peering over the meadows,
The moving stream slowly making its
Way from the shadows,
The trees bare from the cold brazen
Winter,
Hoping for spring, so winter soon
Would end,
Nature unfolding, ever changing, restless,
Yet so free,
The cold, hard mountains mellowed by
The lovely stream, softened by the trees,
Our hearts, often cold and hard as the
Mountains high,
Mellowed by the streams of life, as a
Baby's cry,
Softened by the trees of life, as a mother's song,
No longer as the mountains, so distant and alone.

New Day

The morning sun began to rise, peeking
Over the mountain range.
The water sparkled and danced about,
Welcoming the sun as it came.
A small violet appeared from the green
Grass still damp with dew.
Nature was awaking, stretching forth its
Beauty, as God commanded it to do.

Flowers

Today I watched a flower blossom with
Such array.
Its attire was so gracious, so perfectly
Displayed.
The bee couldn't await the pleasure it
Knew
From sipping the flavor of a blossom that just grew.

Rose

The gentleness of a lovely rose
Awakens a tenderness I hardly know.
A beauty so deep, so truly real,
Alive to nature it makes me feel,
To touch its petals so smooth, so delicate,
Its pose so erect, so much to appreciate—
A beauty so rare is found in the rose.

Sparkling Rose

My heart felt so very tender,
As if for the first time love had enveloped me.
I walked over and gazed from the window;
A rose sparkled from beneath the tender leaves,
With just a small dewdrop trickling down
Its stem.
A tear touched my cheek as I watched.
The rose was pure, lovely, so much like him.
I felt frozen to the view; all time stopped,
For here in a rose was all the love and
Tenderness my mind could attain.
Forever will the beauty and comfort of
Love remain.

God's Enduring Love

God's grace and mercy will always endure,
Although life sometimes is so unsure.
His love is overwhelming, yet so unique.
He gives us strength when we are weak,
Gives us joy when we are sad and lonely,
Hope when despair comes on so suddenly,
A never-ending love as we serve him each day.
Help us, Lord, to walk with you all the way.

Attitudes as Mountains

The cold, hard mountains reach
Above the clouds.
So superior they appear, so confident
And proud,
Never changing as they glare down on
Time and space.
Sometimes our attitudes are as the
Mountains—this we must erase.

Lonely Mountain Peaks

In the distance lie the mountains
Extended to the sky.
Grayish black they look as they lie
Almost out of sight,
Only a silhouette to show that they
Are there never to repeat.
Sometimes our moods are as the
Lonely mountain peaks,
Cold, dark, and alone, judging only what
We see.
Our hearts as heavy as the stones
That lie
High on the mountains
Touching the sky.

Seasons

The flowers bowed their heads;
Their petals began to fall.
They had finished their services.
Nature had made its call.
The trees with limbs outstretched
Relinquished their beauty,
As the leaves floated downward,
Covering the earth as tho their duty.
Summer gives way to autumn as
Autumn to winter,
Winter's death soon defeated as
Spring quietly enters.

To Be Alone

I need to be alone to open up my mind,
To follow down each hallway, thoughts
From other times.
I need to go over all the walls where
Each picture hangs,
See if all the memories are as vivid as
They rang.
I want to separate the bad that seems
Somehow to creep,
To sweep it out from the hallways
Into some deserted street,
To pull from each room the moments
I most cherish,
Hold them securely in my mind, so they
Do not perish,
Check each thought and memory as I go,
To see if as life's road I travel I
Continue to grow.
Let me have the time to be alone and
Open up my mind,
To uncover some new paths as new
Thoughts I find.
I want new hallways, new mountains to explore;
As I embark upon life, give me a challenge,
I implore.

The Longest Day

The day seemed to be extremely long,
So different from the days that had gone.
I felt the pressures of life closing in,
Wishing I could sleep and maybe a new day begin.
But evening was still so far away,
I had first to live out this longest day,
Accept what I could and somehow deal with the rest.
At the close of this day, I must feel I've done
My best.

Taken by the Weeds

So often we cannot see the flowers for
The weeds,
Cannot see the beauty of someone's lovely
Deeds.
Enveloped by this world's ever-growing tensions,
We forget our blessings, so many we cannot mention.
Constant pressures take over our very life;
We then can only feel the drag and strife.
The beauty is still there, only we cannot see,
For our minds are taken, taken by the weeds.

Happiness

Happiness doesn't lie in the things we
Have or places we may go,
Neither in the plans we make or the
Friends we know.
A man I knew had wealth untold, friends
Encamped upon his door,
Yet happiness he had not found—this one
Thing he wanted more.
He made his own way in life, success
Had come, much glamour to follow.
But in the eve his heart was cold and
Empty, his breast lay hollow.
Knowledge could not help this hungry
Man so blind.
Happiness he longed for; he searched, but
Could not find,
For the secret lives within the man.
It's what he does with that which he
Commands.

Peace

The sun came smiling from behind the
Mountains' grandeur
To awake the beauty of this earth, nature
We hold so dear.
The streams sparkled as they rippled neath
The gentle breeze.
Animals slowly ventured out from the
Darkness of the trees.
Flowers glowed with radiance as the tender
Sun descended.
So much beauty, love, joy, and peace
I felt within.

Fall

The earth is slowly changing as each day
Draws to an end.
Wonderful new shades of beauty unfold as
Autumn begins.
Summer with all its wonder steps aside
For the change.
A portrait of calmness is painted as the shades
Of autumn are arranged.

The Cloud

I was covered by a cloud, dark as the darkest sea.
It hovered over, giving no light, no way out for me.
For days the cloud remained, clinging close and tight.
My thinking was distorted, my appearance a fright.
I knew somewhere I had a refuge, a friend.
Somehow I had to get back on track again.
I prayed but my mind could not shake free.
It was lost between this darkness and reality.
Finally, when I could take no more,
I saw a faint light shining through the door.
I grasped this tiny whisper of light,
For I knew this would be my salvation at last.
I felt gratitude for this brightness I'd found,
Gratitude turned to praise and joy did abound.
As the Savior lifted me from beneath the cloud
And placed me in brightness, I was proud,
For inside I had allowed fear and doubt.
Jesus with his loving grace lifted it out.
The doubt brought the cloud, the cloud fear.
Jesus was watching and waiting; it was perfect and
    clear.
Sometimes our lessons seem hard and Jesus stern,
But for future use the lesson must be learned.

Life Is as Vapor

Life is like a vapor that soon disappears,
Leaving only memories of our joys, our hopes, our
     fears:
Each moment should be cherished for it can't be
     relived.
Enjoy life in its complication, that simplicity might
     be revealed.
Be not confined by ignorance nor conform to others'
     ways.
Life is too short to overlook the happiness in each
     moment of the day.

Search for the little things, hold on to
Pleasures, neglecting nothing but giving all,
For life is as a vapor; too soon we'll have
Only memories to recall.
So much happiness can be yours if
You laugh and love and live.

But for the Grace of God

The man, staggering, pulled himself from
The gutter, liquor clasped tightly in his hand,
Desperately holding his bottle, as this was
His courage, his hope, what made him a man.
I watched as he wandered aimlessly down
The narrow, dirty street.
How many, many times a day this sad
Event repeats!
I thought, with grateful tears burning
In my eyes,
But for the grace of God that could be
Me that just passed by.
A deformed child with twisted limbs, a
Half mind, only speaking with a whim,
Afraid, bewildered by what fate
Had bestowed upon him,
The father searching for answers, praying
For wisdom so he might understand,
But for the grace of God I might be that
Child or that man.

Life Is a Book

Life is like a book; each day we fill
A page.
We start when we are born and continue
As we age.
On each page I want a memory of a kind
Deed I've shown:
To walk with the lonely when no one
Else seems to care,
To talk with someone who has a burden
Too great to bear.
Lord, help me to fill my book with love
And understanding,
Not to be selfish to anyone, cruel, or
Demanding.

These are Mine Each Day

Today I had to go down some paths that you couldn't
   go.
I had to say and do some things that you will never
   know,
Had to face some things that were awfully hard to do,
Had to take and give advice; the decisions weren't
   few.
All of these are mine each day, as I proclaim my
   stand.
All made easy because, my dear, you stand behind
   your man.

Thy Love and Saving Grace

I listened to the man as he told of each
Sorrow,
Watched as he talked of dreading each
Tomorrow,
No hope of anything better as he embarked
Upon the day,
Just going on in all his misery; each
Trial seemed the only way.
Watched him as he struggled, each new
Problem seemed to grow—
Soon his body was bending under this
Heavy load.
His mind was a mess of mixed emotions;
Life was unbearable, filled with commotion.
I told him of thy love and saving
Grace.
He couldn't understand, Lord, how your
Son could take his place.

Easy to Forget

Look around you and what do
You see?
Thousands of hungry hearts longing
To be free,
Searching for kindness somewhere
Among the masses,
Tired of being rushed, unnoticed,
Left expressionless.
You had time, but did you forget?
The only smile may be from your lips,
Only a moment to make someone glad.
To be accused so fruitless should
Make you sad,
Yet without notice we complain
And fret.
Yes, so quickly we turn our minds
Inward and we forget.

My Friend

Let the rain fall gently on my skin.
Let the wind softly brush my hair.
As I walk quietly, thanking God for blessings within,
A peace of mind, a thankful heart for those who care,
But, most of all, I'm thankful for *you*, my friend.

Reflections on Childhood

As a child my mind was free to expand,
Not encumbered by pressures of life and its demands.
Protected by my peers, I never felt the rain.
Growing into adulthood, my life began to change.
Disappointments were many; justice
Seemed to have no stand.
Disillusioned by my childhood, I now must take
    command.
The appearance of the moment, whether happy or
    sad,
Would soon disappear leaving only the impression it
    had.
Forgetting sorrow, for brought to mind it will grow,
Now and then reflecting on my childhood to lessen
    the blow.

Working Mother

The house is a mess, the hour at hand.
I must rush out to pick up my man.
Back home again, the supper to fix,
I'll just put something in the oven real quick.
But when I put it on the table so lovely,
I'll ask the Lord to bless it doubly.

The Word Christmas

I love to hear the word Christmas; it means so much
    to me:
The birth of the Baby Jesus who came to set us free.
Long years ago when the Christ Child was born,
Many looked on with hatred and with scorn.
Today let's put away all the hate and malice we might
    feel,
Thinking only of the Christ Child, sharing peace and
    goodwill.